ACHIEVE LEVEL 5

SCIENCE

By **Gerald Page**

RISING STARS

Contents

Section 3:

Answers

How to use this book

1 **Introduction** – This section tells you what you need to do to achieve a Level 5. It picks out the key learning objective and explains it simply to you.

2 **Self-assessment** – Colour in the face that best describes your understanding of this concept.

3 **Question** – The question helps you to learn by doing. It is presented in a similar way to a SATs question and gives you a real example to work with.

4 **Flow chart** – This shows you the steps to use when completing questions like this. Some of the advice appears on every flow chart, such as 'Read the question then read it again'.

 This icon indicates the section is a *teaching* section.

5 **Tip boxes** – These provide test hints and general tips on getting the best marks in the tests.

WHAT WE HAVE INCLUDED:

★ Those topics at Level 4 that are trickiest to get right.

★ ALL Level 5 content so you know that you are covering all the topics that could come up in the test.

★ We have also put in a big selection of our favourite test techniques, tips for revision and some advice on what the tests are all about, as well as the answers so you can see how well you are getting on.

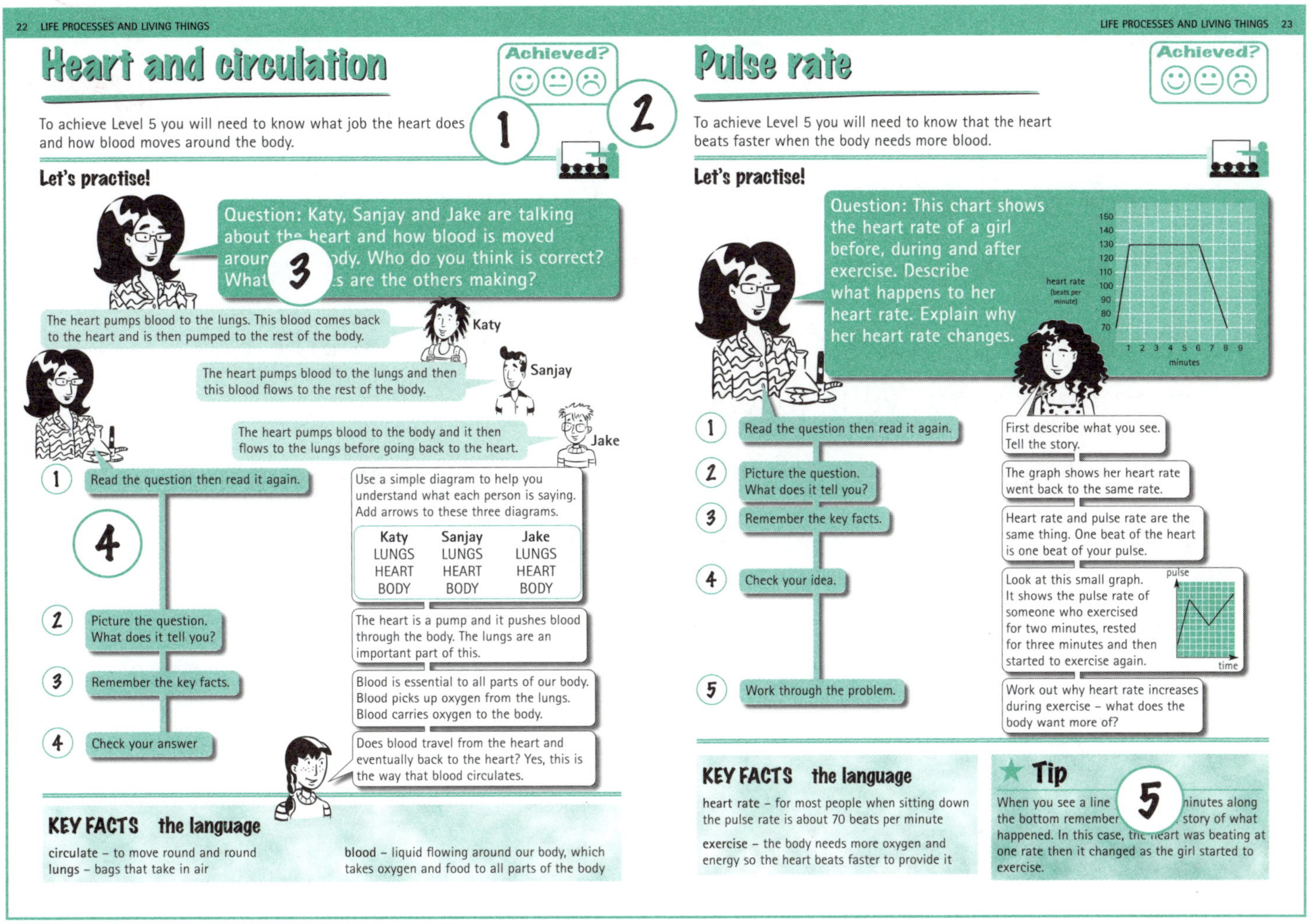

Heart and circulation

Achieved? ☺ ☹ 😐

To achieve Level 5 you will need to know what job the heart does and how blood moves around the body.

Let's practise!

Question: Katy, Sanjay and Jake are talking about the heart and how blood is moved around the body. Who do you think is correct? What ... s are the others making?

The heart pumps blood to the lungs. This blood comes back to the heart and is then pumped to the rest of the body. — **Katy**

The heart pumps blood to the lungs and then this blood flows to the rest of the body. — **Sanjay**

The heart pumps blood to the body and it then flows to the lungs before going back to the heart. — **Jake**

1. Read the question then read it again.

2. Picture the question. What does it tell you?

3. Remember the key facts.

4. Check your answer

Use a simple diagram to help you understand what each person is saying. Add arrows to these three diagrams.

Katy	Sanjay	Jake
LUNGS	LUNGS	LUNGS
HEART	HEART	HEART
BODY	BODY	BODY

The heart is a pump and it pushes blood through the body. The lungs are an important part of this.

Blood is essential to all parts of our body. Blood picks up oxygen from the lungs. Blood carries oxygen to the body.

Does blood travel from the heart and eventually back to the heart? Yes, this is the way that blood circulates.

KEY FACTS   the language

circulate – to move round and round
lungs – bags that take in air

blood – liquid flowing around our body, which takes oxygen and food to all parts of the body

Pulse rate

Achieved? ☺ 😐 ☹

To achieve Level 5 you will need to know that the heart beats faster when the body needs more blood.

Let's practise!

Question: This chart shows the heart rate of a girl before, during and after exercise. Describe what happens to her heart rate. Explain why her heart rate changes.

heart rate (beats per minute) — 150 140 130 120 110 100 90 80 70 — minutes 1 2 3 4 5 6 7 8 9

1. Read the question then read it again.

2. Picture the question. What does it tell you?

3. Remember the key facts.

4. Check your idea.

5. Work through the problem.

First describe what you see. Tell the story.

The graph shows her heart rate went back to the same rate.

Heart rate and pulse rate are the same thing. One beat of the heart is one beat of your pulse.

Look at this small graph. It shows the pulse rate of someone who exercised for two minutes, rested for three minutes and then started to exercise again.

pulse / time

Work out why heart rate increases during exercise – what does the body want more of?

KEY FACTS   the language

heart rate – for most people when sitting down the pulse rate is about 70 beats per minute

exercise – the body needs more oxygen and energy so the heart beats faster to provide it

★ Tip

When you see a line ... minutes along the bottom remember ... story of what happened. In this case, the heart was beating at one rate then it changed as the girl started to exercise.

The National Tests

Key facts

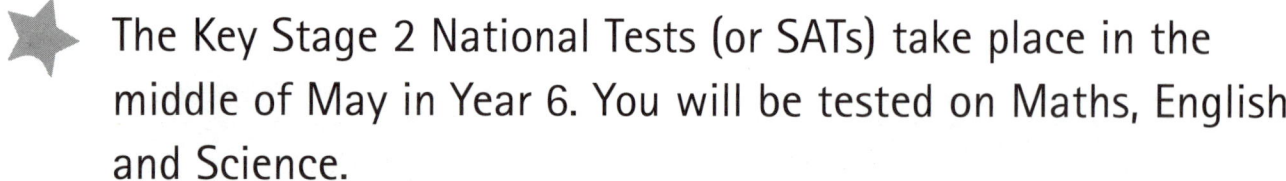

- The Key Stage 2 National Tests (or SATs) take place in the middle of May in Year 6. You will be tested on Maths, English and Science.

- The tests take place in your school and will be marked by examiners – not your teacher!

- You will get your results in July, two months after you take the tests.

- Individual test scores are not made public but a school's combined scores are published in what are commonly known as league tables.

The Science National Tests

You will take two tests in Science each one lasting approximately 45 minutes. These are designed to test your knowledge and skills across the following areas of Science:

- Life processes and living things – the human body, plants and animals and their habitats.

- Materials and their properties – changing different materials, understanding the characteristics of different materials.

- Physical processes – electricity, forces, light and sound, the Sun and the Earth.

DON'T FORGET!

Scientific Enquiry – The National Tests now include more questions that test your *Scientific Enquiry* skills.

The questions will often be based around a picture or a description of an investigation that children have carried out, along with their results. You won't need to carry out the investigation in the test but you might be asked how you would improve it if you were doing the investigation in class.

Recent National Tests papers included questions like:

- Write the question that children were investigating.

- Choose the correct equipment to use in an investigation.

- Complete a table of results from an investigation.

- Draw conclusions from the results of investigations.

- Answer questions about graphs and charts completed in an investigation.

- Describe what children have found out from an investigation.

You might also have to answer some questions about a famous scientist! In 2003 there was a series of questions about Edward Jenner. He found a cure for smallpox a long time ago and saved millions of lives!

ACHIEVE LEVEL 4

Test tips and technique

Before the test

1 When you revise, try revising a 'little and often' rather than in long sessions.

2 Learn the Key Facts (at the end of the book) so that you can recall them instantly. These are your tools for performing your calculations.

3 Revise with a friend. You can encourage and learn from each other.

4 Get a good night's sleep the night before.

5 Make sure you have breakfast!

6 Be prepared – bring your own pens and pencils and wear a watch to check the time as you go.

During the test

1 Don't rush the first few questions. These tend to be quite straightforward, so don't make any silly mistakes.

2 As you know by now, READ THE QUESTION THEN READ IT AGAIN.

3 If you get stuck, don't linger on the same question – move on! You can come back to it later.

4 Never leave a multiple choice question. Guess if you really can't work out the answer.

5 Check to see how many marks a question is worth. Have you 'earned' those marks with your answer?

6 Check your answers after each question. Does your answer look correct?

7 Be aware of the time. After 20 minutes, check to see how far you have got.

8 Try to leave a couple of minutes at the end to read through what you have written.

9 Don't leave any questions unanswered. In the two minutes you have left yourself at the end, make an educated guess at the questions you really couldn't do.

10 Remember, as long as you have done your best, nobody can ask for more. Only you will know if that is the case.

Things to remember

1 Don't panic! If you see a difficult question, take your time, re-read it and have a go!

2 Check every question and every page to be sure you don't miss any! Some questions will want two answers.

3 If a question is about measuring, always write in the UNIT of MEASUREMENT (e.g. newtons, l, kg).

4 Don't be afraid to ask a teacher for anything you need, such as tracing paper or another pencil.

5 Write neatly – if you want to change an answer, put a line through it and write beside the answer box.

6 Always double-check your answers.

Good luck!

Roots, stems and water

At Level 4 you should be able to say how different parts of a plant work.
For example: all plants need water. Water is drawn up from the roots and travels to all parts of the plant through the stem.

Let's practise!

Question: Jim put some red ink in a glass of water. He put a white flower into the water. After a day, there were red patches on the flower. Why do you think there were red marks on the flower?

1 Read the question then read it again.

The flower was white before it went into the water and now it is red.

2 Picture the experiment.

Imagine a similar flower in clear water and another in water with blue ink. What will happen to these?

3 Study the question and make sense of it.

There are no tricks in these questions. It's not possible that Jim simply dripped red ink by accident.

4 Remember the key facts.

Water moves from the roots to all parts of the plant.

5 Work through the problem.

The ink must have travelled up the stem to the flower.

6 Check your answer.

Remember experiments with celery in coloured water. After a few hours the coloured water begins to move up the long thin tubes in the celery stem.

KEY FACTS

water – all living things need it

roots – take water from the soil

stems – water travels up stems from roots

leaves and flowers – need water, which travels up to them

 Tip

In most plants water travels through tiny tubes. It travels from the roots, through the stem and evaporates from the leaves.

Thermal insulators and conductors

Achieved?

At Level 4 you are expected to know that heat passes through some materials more easily than through others.
For example: heat travels more easily through metals than it does through plastic and wood.

Let's practise!

Experiment: Jo puts three spoons in hot water. One spoon is made of wood, one is plastic and one is metal.
● The handle of the metal spoon feels hot.
● The handle of the plastic spoon feels warm.
● The handle of the wooden spoon is not heated at all.
Explain why there is a difference in the heat of the handles.

1. Read the question then read it again.

2. Picture the question. What can you work out?

3. Think about real life examples.

4. Remember the key facts.

5. Work through the problem.

Why is one spoon handle hotter than the others?

The heat must have come from the hot water.

Kettles and pans have plastic or wooden handles to make them easy to touch. Oven gloves stop the heat travelling from very hot objects.

Heat travels through materials.

Heat must travel up the metal and plastic spoons. If it can travel easily through a material then that material is a good conductor.

KEY FACTS   the language

material – what objects are made from

metals – good conductors of heat

plastics – poor conductors of heat

wood – a very poor conductor of heat

CHECK YOUR ANSWER

● A conductor of electricity lets electricity through.

● A conductor of heat lets heat through.

● Good conductors let heat through more easily than poor conductors.

Separating mixtures

Achieved?

At Level 4 you will need to know about the ways to separate simple mixtures.
For example: a salt and water solution.

Let's practise!

Experiment: In some countries people extract salt from seawater. How could you do this?

1 Read the question then read it again.

2 Think about the question. What do you know?

3 Remember the key facts.

4 Work through the problem.

Seawater is a solution of salt and water. To get salt they have to get rid of the water

If you pour a solution of salt and water through a sieve, nothing useful happens. The solution simply goes through the sieve.

Salt dissolves in water. If you let the water evaporate, the salt will be left behind.

If you did this in the classroom, you would
- dissolve the salt in some water
- let the water evaporate
- use the salt

KEY FACTS

dissolve – you cannot see the solid at all because it is in tiny particles in water

solution – a mixture where a solid has dissolved in a liquid

evaporate – this happens when a liquid turns to a gas. This leaves behind any solid that was dissolved.

Other ways to separate mixtures:

sieve – use this to separate most undissolved solids from a liquid, or to separate two solids of different sizes

filter – use this to separate a solution from tiny undissolved pieces

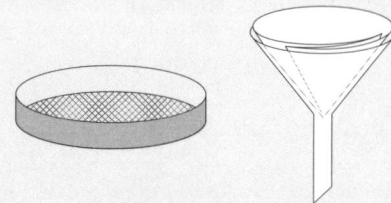

Friction

Achieved?

To reach Level 4 you need to know that forces can stop objects moving. For example: friction can stop cars that are on a slope from rolling.

Let's practise!

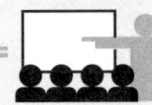

Question: Look at this drawing. The car is parked on a slope. It is not moving. Jim thinks that the car just won't move. Rashid thinks the car won't move because of air resistance acting against it. Sara thinks it will not move because of friction. Who do you think is correct? Why do you think this?

1 Read the question then read it again.

2 Picture the question. Try it out.

3 Think of an everyday example.

4 Work through the problem.

The car is not moving because a force is stopping it.

Put an object on a book and tilt the book. The object begins to slide once the slope is steep.

When a car is parked on a slope it is the friction between the brakes and the wheels that stops it moving.

Gravity is pulling the car down the slope. What force is working against gravity? It cannot be air resistance because air resistance only works when something is moving.

KEY FACTS

gravity – the force that pulls all objects towards the Earth.

friction – the force between two surfaces. It stops things moving or slows down their movement.

air resistance – the force that slows objects as they move through the air.

★ Tip

Gravity works all the time on all objects. Things will fall unless a force stops them. The push from the table stops this book from falling. The push from your chair stops you from falling.

Magnetic attraction and repulsion

Achieved?

At Level 4 you will need to know about how magnets attract and repel one another.

Let's practise!

Experiment: Paula had two bar magnets. Each magnet had a red end and a blue end.
She moved the red and blue ends together and they were attracted. She moved the two blue ends together and found they were repelled. She moved the two red ends together and found they were repelled. Explain what she saw.

1 Read the question then read it again.

Notice the words **attract** and **repel**. Attract means the magnets were pulled together. Repel means they were pushed apart.

2 Picture the question. What does it tell you?

There is a force pushing **like** ends apart. There is a force pulling **unlike** ends together.

3 Think about magnetic poles.

The red and blue ends are called the **poles** of the magnet. The red pole is always the north pole of the magnet and the blue end is the south pole of the magnet.

4 Remember the key facts.

Like poles repel and unlike poles attract.

5 Work through the problem.

Unlike magnetic poles attract. Like magnetic poles repel.

 Tip

Always use the correct words when talking about magnets:
Poles are the ends of the magnet.
Attract is the correct word. Do not say stick.
Repel is the correct word for push apart.

Magnetic sorting

Achieved?

At Level 4 you will need to know which metals are magnetic and which are not.

Let's practise!

Question: Ravi tests materials to see which are attracted to a magnet. He sorts them into two sets.
All of the set that are attracted to magnets are metal.
He lists the different metals.

metal	used for	Does it conduct electricity?	Is it attracted to magnets?
aluminium	drinks cans	yes	no
steel	many food cans	yes	yes
copper	wires	yes	no
gold	rings	yes	no
iron	railings	yes	yes

List the metals that are magnetic and list the metals that are not magnetic.

Metals attracted to magnets	Metals not attracted to magnets

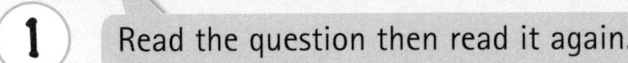

1. Read the question then read it again.

No non-metals are magnetic. Some metals are attracted to magnets.

2. Picture the question. What does it tell you?

All you have to do is write two lists.

3. Think of an everyday example.

Iron and steel are the only magnetic metals shown on the list.

4. Work through the problem.

HINTS

- When testing metals, if one is attracted to a magnet, **it must have iron or steel in it.** Tin cans only have a very thin layer of tin over an inside of steel.

- Find out as much as you can about types of metals and what they are used for.

Patterns in data

At Level 4 you will need to be able to interpret patterns in data.
For example: interpreting a bar chart.

Let's practise!

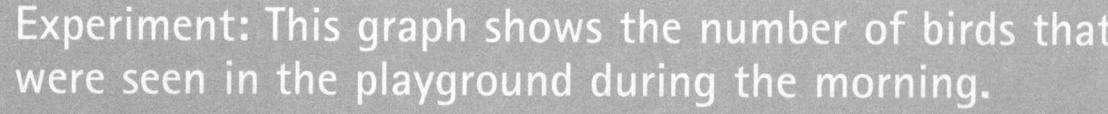

Experiment: This graph shows the number of birds that were seen in the playground during the morning.

Number of birds

50
40
30
20
10

09.00   09.30   10.00   10.30   11.00

Time

At what time were there most birds in the playground?
At what time were there fewest birds in the playground?

1 Read the question then read it again.

2 Picture the question. What does it tell you?

3 Remember the key facts.

4 Work through the problem.

You are only being asked to say what the chart shows.

The time is written along the bottom and the number of birds up the side.

The taller columns show more birds.

Most birds were in the playground at 11.00. Fewest birds were in the playground at 10.30.

KEY FACTS

There are three main types of graphs and charts.

Bar chart The taller the column, the greater the amount.

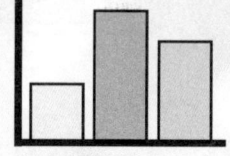

Pie chart The bigger the piece of pie, the greater the amount.

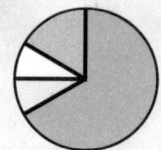

Line graph The higher the line goes, the greater the amount.

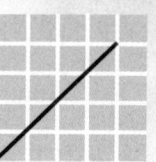

Explaining patterns in data

Achieved?

At Level 4 you will need to be able to explain patterns in data.
For example: explaining why one factor depends on another.

Let's practise!

Question: Look at this chart. It shows the distance that a toy car travelled along a table after it left a ramp. Yasmin noticed that when the ramp was very steep the car bumped on the table when it left the ramp. Explain the pattern you see in the chart.

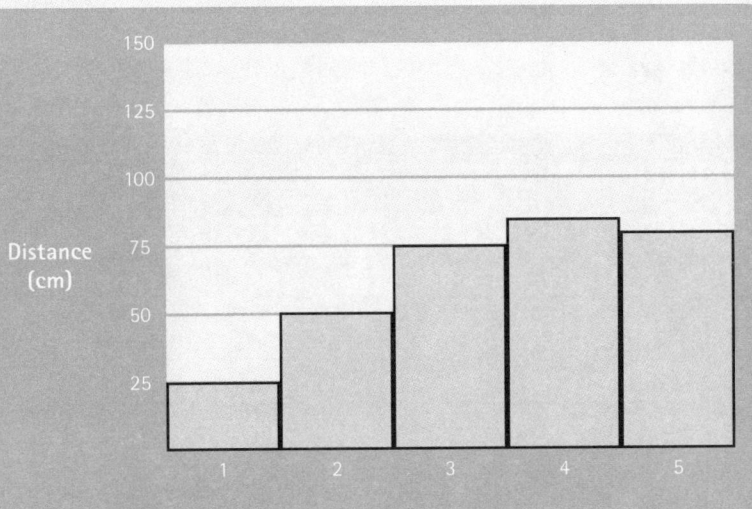

Distance (cm)

150
125
100
75
50
25

1   2   3   4   5

Number of blocks under ramp

1 Read the question then read it again.

2 Picture the question. What does it tell you?

3 Remember the key facts.

4 Work through the problem.

This time you are being asked to explain the bar chart and not simply describe it.

Five heights of ramp were tried.

The taller the bar on the chart, the further the car went, except for the last ramp height.

The distance travelled depends on the height of the ramp. The car travelled further as the ramp got steeper, until the last ramp height. The car must have bumped onto the table when it left the ramp. This must have slowed it down, so it did not travel as far.

★ **Tip**

Look for the patterns and describe them first. If there is a change in the pattern, think of a reason why the change could have happened.

Scientific enquiry spotting problem results

Achieved?

To reach Level 4 you will need to be able to spot results that are probably wrong.

Let's practise!

Experiment: Jim and Sue were using an elastic band to catapult a toy car along a track. They measured how far back they pulled the elastic band.

They measured how far the car went.

a) Explain the pattern of most of the results.

b) Circle the one result which was probably a mistake.

c) Explain why you think it is a mistake.

How far the band was pulled back	How far the car travelled		
	1st try	2nd try	3rd try
2 cm	30	34	56
4 cm	41	40	38
6 cm	62	60	59

1 Read the question then read it again.

You have to explain the pattern. This means you will have to say what you expect to happen as the band is pulled further back. You only need to circle one result in question (b).

2 Picture the question.

Look at the pattern of the results – you would expect similar results on each try.

3 Remember the key facts.

Distance travelled depends on the amount the band is pulled back.

4 Work through the problem.

The pattern of the results shows that the further back you pull the band the further the car travels.

The mistake was the 56 cm result. It was much higher than the other results for the same pullback. It was further than the result for 4 cm pullback.

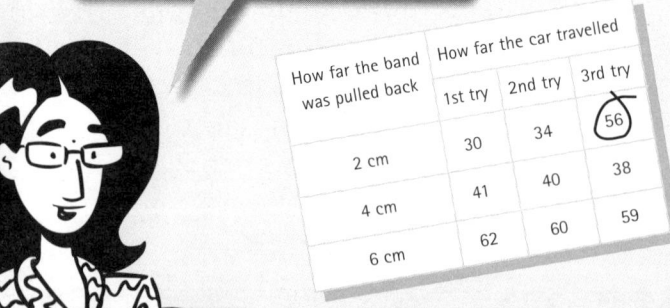

How far the band was pulled back	How far the car travelled		
	1st try	2nd try	3rd try
2 cm	30	34	(56)
4 cm	41	40	38
6 cm	62	60	59

KEY FACTS   the language

pattern – look for a sequence of results.
Look for increases or decreases.

Scientific enquiry variables

To reach Level 4 you will need to be able to say which variables you will change, which you will measure and which you will keep the same.

Let's practise!

Shefqat is seeing how many seeds germinate from different packets of seed.	Julie is seeing how various exercises affect her pulse rate.	Tim is doing an experiment to see if the temperature of water affects the speed at which salt dissolves.
Circle the variables that you would keep the same in this experiment.	Circle the variables that you would alter in this experiment.	Circle the variables that you would measure in this experiment.
Variables ● the compost ● speed of germination ● the temperature ● the type of seed	**Variables** ● Julie's pulse rate ● the type of exercise she does ● how she measures her pulse rate	**Variables** ● the temperature of the water ● the time taken to dissolve ● the amount of salt at the start

1 Read the question then read it again.

The words are really important here.

2 Remember the key facts.

What you keep the same are the variables that do not affect anything. In most experiments, you try to alter only one thing at a time and then try to measure the changes that occur.

3 Work through the problem.

For Shefqat's experiment you circle 'compost' and 'temperature' because those two factors should be the same for each type of seed to ensure the test is fair.	For Julie's experiment you circle the type of exercise because she wants to see how this single factor affects her pulse rate.	For Tim's experiment you circle them all. He wants to measure the thing that has the effect (the temperature) and what effect it has (time taken to dissolve). He will need to check that the amount of salt at the start is the same.

Function of human organs

Achieved?

To achieve Level 5 you will need to know the main functions of human organs.
For example: the heart, brain and lung functions.

Let's practise!

Question: What are the main functions of the heart, the lungs and the brain?

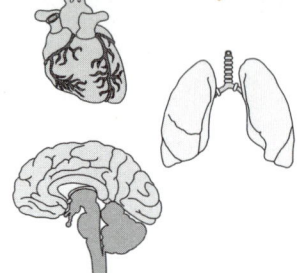

heart	
lungs	
brain	

1 Read the question then read it again.

Function means the job something does. An organ is part of the body with a special job to do.

2 Picture the human body.

Think about where these organs are located.

3 Study the question and make sense of it.

The lungs and heart are very close to each other.

4 Remember the key facts.

- Lungs draw in air.
- Heart pumps blood.
- Blood carries oxygen to all parts of the body.
- Brain controls movement and thinking.

5 Work through the problem.

List the functions next to the name of the organ.

6 Check your answer.

Use the word **pump** to describe the heart.

KEY FACTS   the language

blood – liquid that carries food and oxygen to the body
air – mixture of gases that we breathe
oxygen – the gas in air that our bodies need
carbon dioxide – the gas we breathe out

Plant organs

To achieve Level 5 you will need to know the main functions of plant organs.
For example: the reproductive parts of a flower.

Let's practise!

Question: What are the main organs of a flowering plant and what are their functions?

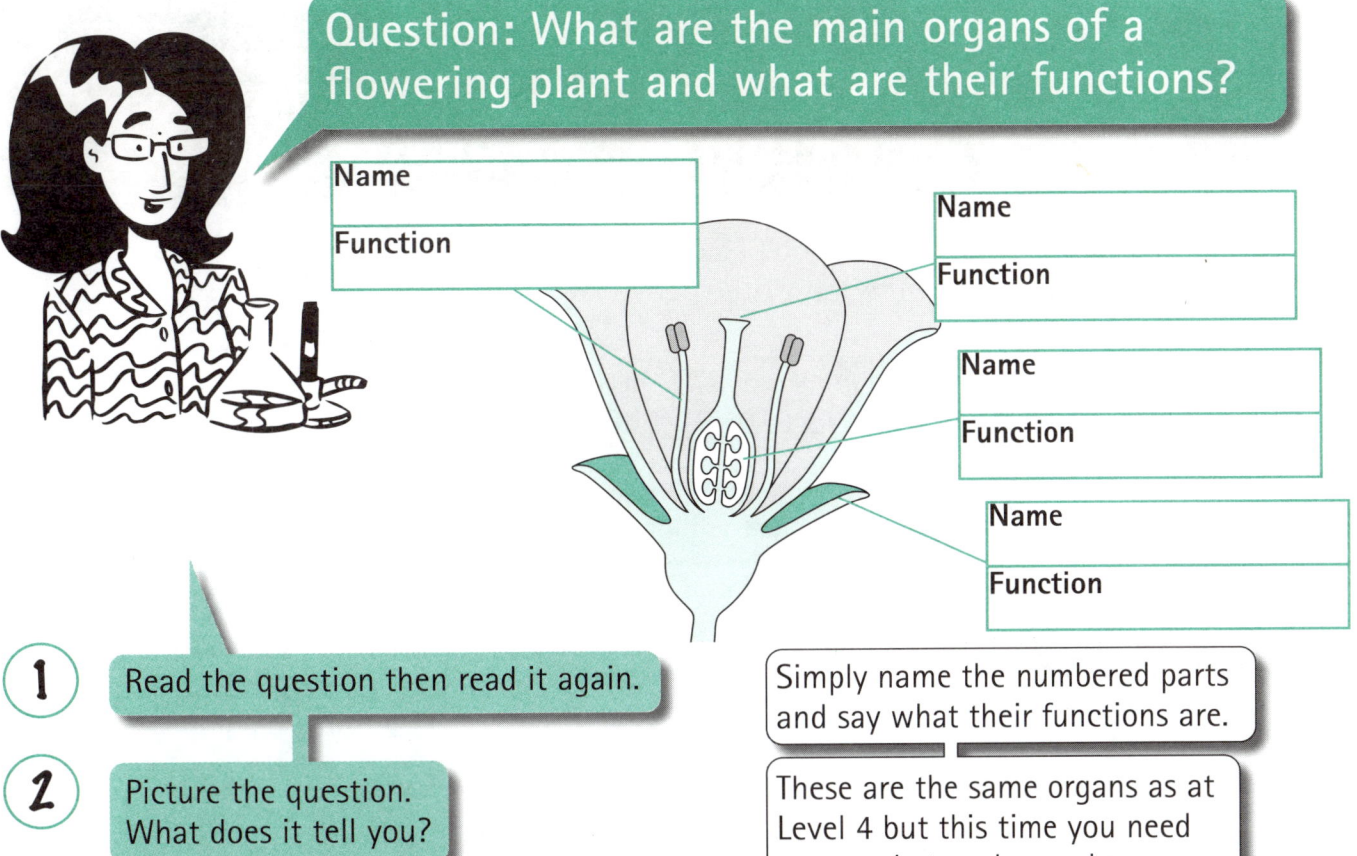

Name

Function

Name

Function

Name

Function

Name

Function

① Read the question then read it again.

Simply name the numbered parts and say what their functions are.

② Picture the question. What does it tell you?

These are the same organs as at Level 4 but this time you need to say what each one does.

③ Remember the key facts.

Flowers are there to produce seeds. Seeds develop from ovules in the ovary. Seeds are pollinated when male pollen from the stamen lands on the stigma. The pollen travels down to the ovules to make seeds.

④ Work through the problem.

Start by deciding which parts are male and which are female.

KEY FACTS

stigma – the female part where pollen sticks
stamen – the male parts, which produce pollen
ovule – undeveloped seed

ovary – the box that contains the ovule and later the seeds
seed – an object produced by a plant, which may eventually grow into another plant
petals – colourful outer part of flower

★ **Tip**

StigMA is female
StaMEN is male

Heart and circulation

To achieve Level 5 you will need to know what job the heart does and how blood moves around the body.

Let's practise!

Question: Katy, Sanjay and Jake are talking about the heart and how blood is moved around the body. Who do you think is correct? What mistakes are the others making?

The heart pumps blood to the lungs. This blood comes back to the heart and is then pumped to the rest of the body.

Katy

The heart pumps blood to the lungs and then this blood flows to the rest of the body.

Sanjay

The heart pumps blood to the body and it then flows to the lungs before going back to the heart.

Jake

① Read the question then read it again.

Use a simple diagram to help you understand what each person is saying. Add arrows to these three diagrams.

Katy	Sanjay	Jake
LUNGS	LUNGS	LUNGS
HEART	HEART	HEART
BODY	BODY	BODY

② Picture the question. What does it tell you?

The heart is a pump and it pushes blood through the body. The lungs are an important part of this.

③ Remember the key facts.

Blood is essential to all parts of our body. Blood picks up oxygen from the lungs. Blood carries oxygen to the body.

④ Check your answer

Does blood travel from the heart and eventually back to the heart? Yes, this is the way that blood circulates.

KEY FACTS   the language

circulate – to move round and round
lungs – bags that take in air

blood – liquid flowing around our body, which takes oxygen and food to all parts of the body

Pulse rate

To achieve Level 5 you will need to know that the heart beats faster when the body needs more blood.

Let's practise!

Question: This chart shows the heart rate of a girl before, during and after exercise. Describe what happens to her heart rate. Explain why her heart rate changes.

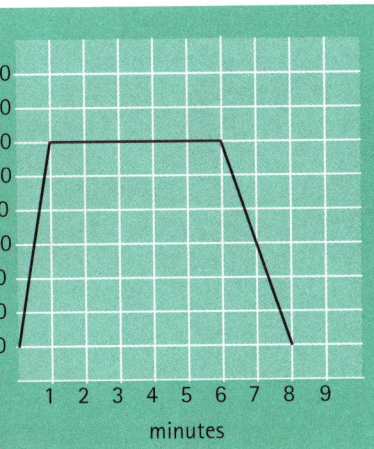

heart rate
(beats per minute)

150
140
130
120
110
100
90
80
70

1 2 3 4 5 6 7 8 9

minutes

1 Read the question then read it again.

First describe what you see. Tell the story.

2 Picture the question. What does it tell you?

The graph shows her heart rate went back to the same rate.

3 Remember the key facts.

Heart rate and pulse rate are the same thing. One beat of the heart is one beat of your pulse.

4 Check your idea.

Look at this small graph. It shows the pulse rate of someone who exercised for two minutes, rested for three minutes and then started to exercise again.

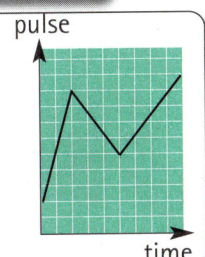

pulse

time

5 Work through the problem.

Work out why heart rate increases during exercise – what does the body want more of?

KEY FACTS   the language

heart rate – for most people when sitting down the pulse rate is about 70 beats per minute

exercise – the body needs more oxygen and energy so the heart beats faster to provide it

⭐ Tip

When you see a line graph with minutes along the bottom remember to tell the story of what happened. In this case, the heart was beating at one rate then it changed as the girl started to exercise.

Animal life cycles

Achieved?

To achieve Level 5 you will need to know the life cycles of different animals.
For example: the changes in an insect as it develops.

Let's practise!

Question: Describe the main parts of the life cycle of a butterfly.

1 Read the question then read it again.

2 Picture the question. What does it tell you?

3 Remember the key facts.

4 Work through the problem.

5 Check your answer.

First, list the stages in the life cycle of a butterfly and then describe each one.

Draw each stage in a circle with arrows connecting the stages.

Study the stages in the life cycle of different animals, such as frogs and bluebottles. How are humans and other mammals different or similar?

All animals are born and grow old and die. They all go through stages. In humans and other mammals, several of the stages happen inside the mother's body before birth.

When you have written the names of the stages, write in what happens at each stage.

KEY FACTS   the language

egg – all animals start as eggs. You started as an egg inside your mother.

caterpillar – in butterflies the egg hatches into a caterpillar. Caterpillars are like miniature leaf-eating machines! Not all insects have a caterpillar stage.

pupa – the caterpillar makes a covering around itself while it changes into an adult butterfly

adult – at this stage the butterfly mates, lays eggs and dies

 **Tip**

The frog life cycle is similar to the butterfly in many ways, but it does not make a pupa.

In mammals the young is born looking like a very small adult.

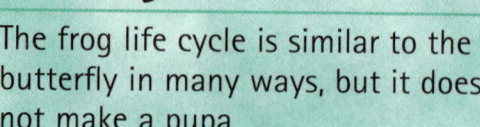

Plant life cycles

Achieved?

To achieve Level 5 you will need to know the main stages in a plant's life cycle.
For example: the stages of pollination and seed dispersal.

Let's practise!

Question: These stages in the life cycle of a flowering plant are mixed up. Number them in the correct order starting with germination.

- growing plant ⬜
- dispersal of seeds ⬜
- flowering ⬜

- development of seeds ⬜
- pollination ⬜
- germination of seed **1**

① Read the question then read it again.

② Picture the question. Think about what you know.

③ Remember the key facts.

④ Check your answer.

Decide where to start from. It is probably best to start with growing plant.

The cycle of a plant is similar to that of an animal. It grows, mates, produces seeds and dies.

Pollination and germination are two different processes. Pollination happens when male pollen meets the female ovule and makes a seed.

Read through the list – picture each stage and what went before.

KEY FACTS

pollination – the process where pollen from the male part of the plant fertilises the female ovule to make a seed

germination – the process where a seed sprouts and starts growing

Tip

Think about a particular flower, such as a dandelion. You see the bright yellow flower before the fluffy seeds are formed.

Keys

To achieve Level 5 you will need to be able to work out the names of living things using keys.

Let's practise!

Question: Name the twigs A and B.

A
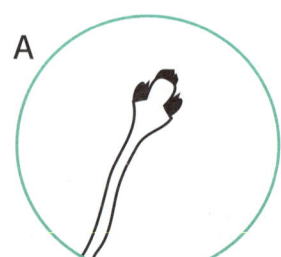

B
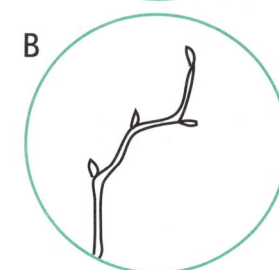

Are the buds in pairs opposite each other?

- **yes**
  Are the buds black?
  - **yes**
    ash
  - **no**
    sycamore
- **no**
  Are the buds in groups at the end of the twig?
  - **yes**
    oak
  - **no**
    lime

1 Read the question then read it again.

You probably do not know the answer straight away so try to work it out logically. Look at the twig labelled A. Answer the questions in the key based on that twig.

2 Picture the question.

Start at the beginning. Answer the first question in the sequence. There are two pathways. Choose the answers that match twig A.

3 Remember the key facts.

Buds opposite each other are in pairs on either side of the twig.

4 Check your answer.

Now answer the questions based on twig B.
You should end up with a different answer from twig A.

KEY FACTS   the language

twig – thin part at the end part of a branch.
bud – tightly folded leaves and flowers. In winter these are protected by bud scales.

Buds are often set out in pairs opposite each other down the twig. There is usually a single bud at the very end of the twig.

★ Tip

All keys work like this one. Once you understand this one you will be able to use most keys.

Classification

To achieve Level 5 you will need to classify living things into groups.
For example: animals with backbones.

Let's practise!

Question: Here is some information about five kinds of animal:

- **mammal** – gives birth to live young and feeds young on milk
- **bird** – has feathers and lays eggs
- **reptile** – has dry scaly skin and lays eggs on land
- **amphibian** – has damp skin and lays eggs in water
- **fish** – lives in water and has gills

List these animals and say which group each one belongs to.

seagull	snake	frog	shark	lizard
human	toad	penguin	pike	cow

(Clue: there are two of each kind.)

1 Read the question then read it again.

Start to put the animals in pairs that seem similar.

2 Picture the question. What do you know?

Read about each kind of animal and think about the skin each has. Fish can be tricky as some are scaly and some are not. Mammals can be difficult as some appear hairy and others do not.

3 Remember the key facts.

These are all in the question – the description of each animal type.

4 Work through the problem.

If you end up with three in one group, one of them must be wrong.

5 Check your answer.

Think of another example of each animal type.

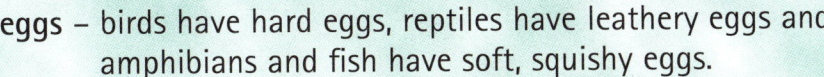

KEY FACTS   the language

eggs – birds have hard eggs, reptiles have leathery eggs and amphibians and fish have soft, squishy eggs.

hair – mammals, like humans, only have noticeable hair in a few parts of their body. Whales do not appear to have hair.

scales – made of a material like your fingernail.

Habitats

Achieved?

To achieve Level 5 you will need to know the ways in which different animals and plants are suited to different habitats.
For example: some animals like dark and damp places.

Let's practise!

Question: A group of children were studying woodlice. They found out that woodlice liked damp and dark conditions and ate rotting plants. They looked for woodlice in their school grounds. They looked in four different places. This table shows the number they found.

In the playground	Under a piece of old carpet	In the long grass	Under a rotting log
0	13	2	44

Explain these results

1 Read the question then read it again.

2 Picture the question. What does it tell you?

3 Remember the key facts.

4 Check your answer.

There were far more woodlice under the log than anywhere else. There were quite a few under the carpet.

The woodlice seemed to need two things in the places they live – food and shelter.

Woodlice are small animals that need damp and dark conditions.
They feed on rotting plants.

Plan a home for woodlice in your classroom. What things would you need to provide for them?

KEY FACTS   the language

habitat – the place where an animal or plant lives

environment – what the conditions in a habitat are like.

conditions – what a place is like. Is it damp or dry? Is it hot or cold?

★ Tip

All animals and plants live in habitats that suit them. If the conditions do not give them what they need, they will die.

A bird's habitat might be gardens or woods. Just because birds spend a lot of time in their nest does not mean that their nest is their habitat.

Environments

To achieve Level 5 you will need to know the ways that some animals and plants are suited to their environment.

For example: some plants have a number of ways of conserving water.

Let's practise!

Question: Look at this cactus plant. In what ways is it suited to its environment? Finish off the sentences with one of these endings:

water evaporating   make food

store water   water from the soil

animals eating the plant

spikes

tough outer skin

swollen stems

green stem

deep roots

Tough outer skin to stop _____

Spikes to stop _____

Deep roots to get _____

Green stem to _____

Swollen stems to _____

1. Read the question then read it again.

2. Picture the question. What does it tell you?

3. Remember the key facts.

4. Think about another example.

Think about a cactus and the way it survives in the desert.

The endings can only be used once. Some could fit in more than one place but there is one solution that works best.

Cacti need to get water. They need to avoid losing water. They need to stop animals from eating them.

How are worms suited to their environment? They have a long thin body, they are slimy to slide through the soil and they eat decaying plants in the soil.

KEY FACTS   the language

environment – what a place is like.

food – plants normally make food in their leaves. Cacti use their green stems to make food.

Competition for light and water

Achieved?

To achieve Level 5 you will need to show you understand how plants and animals get enough light and water to grow and breed.

Let's practise!

Question: Deciduous trees do not have leaves in winter and only small, new leaves in spring. In a deciduous wood in spring the ground is covered with bluebells and many other types of small flowers. In summer all these plants die down and there is mainly bare ground. Explain why this happens.

1 Read the question then read it again.

The question is asking about the reason why small plants only grow under trees in spring. Why do they die down in summer when most other plants are growing best?

2 Picture the question. What does it tell you?

In spring there are only small, new leaves on the trees. In summer there are lots of tree leaves cutting out light.

3 Remember the key facts.

Bluebells would not get enough light in the summer because of the shade of the tree leaves. Bluebells grow from bulbs.

4 Think of other examples like this.

In the spring bulbs such as daffodils grow in grass. Once the grass starts to grow the daffodils shrivel back and wait until next spring to grow.

KEY FACTS   the language

deciduous – trees and other woody plants that lose their leaves

bulbs – stores of energy that let a plant start growing when it is too cold and dark for most other plants to grow

 Tip

You do not need to know much about plants to work this one out. It is all about one type of plant starting to grow before the others have woken up. They can only do this with a ready-made food store. They use their leaves to refill their food store just before the other plants overgrow them.

Burning

To achieve Level 5 you will need to know that some materials burn when they are heated.
For example: some materials only melt, while others melt and then burn. Another group burns without melting.

Let's practise!

Question: Tan's teacher heated different materials over a candle flame.

paper   sugar   cotton   cheese   salt   nylon

The class put them into three different groups:
Melt then burn   Burn without melting   No change

Which group will you put each material into?

Melt then burn	Burn without melting	No change

1. Read the question then read it again.

2. Think of everyday examples.

3. Work through the problem.

Look at each material and decide what would happen to it.

When you leave bread in the toaster too long, it will burn. It is very dangerous to heat a chip pan for too long because it will suddenly burn. If you heat marshmallows on a barbecue, they go drippy and will burn if they fall into the fire.

Which materials will not change?

KEY FACTS   the language

melt – turn from a solid into a liquid

burn – catch fire

★ Tip

When a material burns it produces new materials. Toast that burns turns into black carbon. The smoke that comes off burning toast is a new material too.

Fizzing mixtures

Achieved?

To achieve Level 5 you will need to know that some mixtures produce gas.
For example: vinegar and baking powder produce a gas when they are mixed.

Let's practise!

Question: Andy's teacher had two small bottles.
He put water and salt into one of the bottles.
After a short time the salt disappeared. He put vinegar and baking powder into the other bottle.
The mixture fizzed and bubbled.
What happened to the salt in the water?
Why do you think the second mixture fizzed and bubbled?
Which of the two changes would be most difficult to reverse?

water   salt

vinegar   baking powder

1 Read the question then read it again.

Think about the changes that made the second mixture fizz and bubble. The first mixture is much simpler – the salt dissolved in the water.

2 What is similar in everyday life?

To make cakes we add baking powder to our mix. This makes bubbles, which get bigger in the oven and make the cake light and fluffy. Yeast makes bubbles in bread dough, which makes the holes in bread. Sugar dissolves in water.

3 Remember the key facts.

There is a change happening in the bubbling mixture that is very difficult to reverse. The chemical reaction between the baking powder and the vinegar produces a gas.

KEY FACTS   the language

reversible change – a change that can be easily reversed

dissolving – a change that is easy to reverse

fizzing – this happens in a mixture when a gas is produced

★ Tip

Chemical changes are not easy to reverse because they produce a new substance.

Evaporation

Achieved?

To achieve Level 5 you will need to know that evaporation takes place in a variety of conditions.
For example: heat increases the speed of evaporation.

Let's practise!

Question: Kamal put 100 ml of water in three identical jars. He put each one in a different place.

On a hot radiator / In a cool place / On a table in a warm room

A day later he checked how much water was in each jar.
What happened to the water?
Explain why some jars had less water in than others.

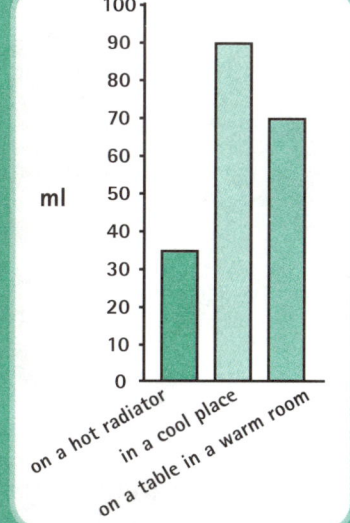

ml — bar chart with values 100, 90, 80, 70, 60, 50, 40, 30, 20, 10, 0
on a hot radiator / in a cool place / on a table in a warm room

1 Read the question then read it again.

2 Picture the question. What can you work out?

3 Remember the key facts.

4 Work through the problem.

Each jar started with the same amount of water. After a time some of the water in each jar had gone.

Water has turned to a gas and gone into the air.

When a liquid turns to gas it is called evaporation.

Why did less water evaporate from one container than another? Heat was involved. When there was more heat, more water evaporated.

KEY FACTS   the language

evaporate – turn from a liquid to a gas

⭐ Tip

Liquids evaporate more quickly when:

- it is warm

- there is a breeze blowing

Condensation

To achieve Level 5 you will need to know the conditions in which condensation takes place.
For example: the water vapour in air condenses on cold surfaces.

Let's practise!

Annie looked at her reflection in the bathroom mirror. She had a bath. When she got out, she noticed the mirror was completely misted up.

Lee took a can of drink out of the fridge. He did not open it. Soon after he put it on the table, water was running down the outside of the can.

Explain what was happening in both cases.

1. Read the question then read it again.

2. Picture the question. What can you work out?

3. Think of similar examples.

4. Think through what is happening.

Something similar was happening in both cases.

The water must have come from the air.

When you breathe on a mirror, it mists up. In cold weather, water runs down the inside of windows.

Water vapour is in the air all the time. It changes to liquid water when it is cool. The air near the can is cooled. The mirror is cooler than the hot air in the bathroom.

KEY FACTS   the language

water vapour – water in a gas form
condensation – the change from gas to liquid

★ Tip 1

Use the correct word – condenses rather than mists up.

★ Tip 2

Clouds are masses of tiny drops of liquid water that have condensed in the cold of the upper atmosphere.

Change of state

To achieve Level 5 you will need to know that materials can change state.
For example: liquids turn to solids when they cool. They turn to gases
when heated.

Let's practise!

Sam put some sugar in a spoon. He held the spoon with a wooden peg. He heated the spoon over a candle flame. The sugar melted and bubbled.

John used a candle flame to heat water in a spoon. He waited as it boiled away.

Jane poured water from the tap into an ice cube maker and put it in the freezer for a day.

Which person watched the following changes of state?

Write their names in the correct place.

person watching	change
	solidifying
	evaporating
	melting

1. Read the question then read it again.

2. Remember the key facts.

3. Work through the problem.

You need to match the person to the change of state.

A liquid evaporates when it turns into a gas.
A liquid solidifies when it turns into a solid.
A solid melts when it turns into a liquid.

Now write in the name of the correct person.

KEY FACTS – the language

liquid **solidify** ➤ solid   liquid **evaporate** ➤ gas   solid **melt** ➤ liquid

Separating mixtures

Achieved?

At Level 5 you will need to know about the ways to separate mixtures.
For example: mixtures where one part needs to be dissolved and then filtered.

Let's practise!

Question: Kate has been given a mixture of instant coffee granules and sand. She has been asked to separate the two solids. Describe how she should separate the solids.

1 Read the question then read it again.

2 Remember the key facts.

3 Work through the problem.

4 Complete the experiment.

5 Think about other examples.

It is a strange mixture but you need to get the two solids apart. Sieving won't help as the coffee and sand particles are about the same size.

Filters let liquids and dissolved solids through.

If you add water to the mixture, the coffee will dissolve. The solution of coffee and water will go through a filter but the sand will not.

Let the water evaporate leaving the coffee behind.

Other mixtures that could be separated in this way are sand and salt or sugar and sand. How would you separate
● steel staples and sand?
● wax and sand?

Ways to separate mixtures:

sieve   use this to separate most undissolved solids from a liquid, or to separate two solids of different sizes

filter   use this to separate a solution from tiny undissolved pieces

KEY FACTS   the language

dissolve – you cannot see the solid at all because it is in tiny particles in liquid

solution – a mixture where a solid has dissolved in a liquid

evaporate – this happens when a liquid turns to a gas. This leaves behind any dissolved solid.

Metals

Achieved?

To achieve Level 5 you will need to know the main properties of metals.
For example: all metals conduct electricity but only a few are attracted to magnets.

Let's practise!

Question: Rey tested some materials. Two of the materials are metals. He made a table showing their properties.

Sample	Colour	Does it conduct electricity?	Is it magnetic?
A	grey	yes	yes
B	white	no	no
C	yellow	yes	no
D	green	no	no

Which are most likely to be metals?

One of the metals is gold. The other is iron.

Iron is sample ☐   Gold is sample ☐

1 Read the question then read it again.

The table has all the information you need.

2 Picture the question. What does it tell you?

Two of the samples conduct electricity. One of the samples conducts electricity AND is magnetic.

3 Remember the key facts.

All metals conduct electricity. Iron and steel are the only common magnetic metals.

4 Work through the problem.

Do the first part. Then decide which description matches iron best.

5 Check your answer.

Iron conducts electricity and is magnetic. Gold conducts electricity but is not magnetic.

KEY FACTS   the language

conducts electricity – lets electricity through

magnetic – attracted to a magnet

★ Tip

You don't need to know about the other two materials but they could be plastics of some kind.

Uses of metals

Achieved?

To achieve Level 5 you will need to know the main properties of metals.
For example: different metals are suited to different uses.

Let's practise!

Question: Use this table to answer the questions.

Metal	Is it expensive?	Does it rust?	Is it strong?	Is it strong and light?
steel	no	yes	yes	no
stainless steel	yes	no	yes	no
platinum	yes	no	no	no
aluminium	no	no	yes	yes

a) Which metal is used to make strong knives and forks that will not rust?

b) Motorcars need a strong body that is cheap. What two metals could be used to make cars?

c) Why are planes usually made from aluminium?

d) Why would you not use platinum to make baked bean tins?

1 Read the question then read it again.

2 What can you work out?

3 Study the table for clues.

4 Think about everyday examples.

Do one question at a time.

All the information is in the table.

Each metal has a different set of properties.

Look at the knives and forks you eat with. They are smooth and shiny. Look at the writing on them... it is almost certain to say 'stainless'. Most cars are made from steel that has been painted to stop it going rusty. Aluminium is used to make very fast cars – this is because aluminium is a light metal.

KEY FACTS   metal properties

Metals are a very varied group of materials.

- Aluminium and titanium are very light.

- Gold and lead are very heavy.

- Lead and gold both melt at low temperatures.

- Tungsten is the metal in light bulb filaments. It melts at very high temperatures.

- Steel cans are coated with a very thin layer of tin. Tin is an expensive metal.

- Rare metals like gold and platinum are used for jewellery.

Candle wax changes

Achieved?

To achieve Level 5 you will need to know about the properties of materials.

Let's practise!

Question: James lit a candle weighing 10 g. After an hour, he noticed that it had become smaller. The candle now weighed 6 g.

Explain why the candle weighs less after it has been burning for an hour.

What changes have taken place? Are these changes easy to reverse?

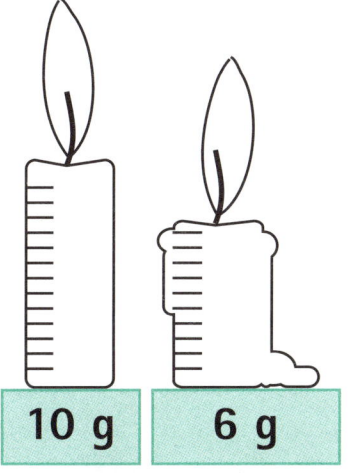

10 g   **6 g**

1. Read the question then read it again.

2. Picture the question. What does it tell you?

3. Remember the key facts.

4. Work through the problem.

The candle weighs less after it has been burning – what has happened to the weight?

There is much less wax than there was. The wax must have been burnt.

Wax burns and forms new materials. These new materials are gases.

Changes like this are difficult to reverse. This is an example of a chemical change.

SCIENCE BACKGROUND

When lighting a candle the match melts some wax. The wick soaks up the liquid wax. It then evaporates off the wick. The wax gas then burns and makes new materials called carbon dioxide and water. Both these new materials are in the form of gases.

Wood burns and changes

Achieved?

To achieve Level 5 you will need to know the main properties of materials. For example: wood is a fuel. When it is burnt the wood is changed into new materials. These new materials are difficult to turn back into wood.

Let's practise!

Question: On bonfire night the children saw a large pile of wood for the fire. The next day they saw that the pile of wood was still smoking and was much smaller.

Matt thinks the wood had packed down.

Julie thinks some of the wood changed into a gas when it was burnt.

Hannah thinks that the wood had just turned to ash because of the heat.

a) Which of these children is correct?

b) Explain your idea.

1 Read the question then read it again.

2 Picture the question. What do you know?

3 Work through the problem.

The three children each have a different idea.

Burning wood is the same as burning candle wax. The wood is a fuel just like the candle wax is the fuel for the candle.

When a fuel burns it produces new materials. These new materials are gases.

KEY FACT

Ash is the unburnt, solid part of the wood. The weight of the ash left in the fire is much less than the weight of the wood they started with.

Circuit symbols

To achieve Level 5 you will need to know the symbols for electrical devices.
For example: the symbols for battery, bulb, switch and buzzer in a circuit.

battery   bulb   switch   buzzer

Let's practise!

> **Question: a)** Draw two circuits that show two bulbs with a switch and a battery.
> - Draw one of the circuits with the switch on.
> - Draw the other circuit with the switch off.
>
> **b)** Draw another circuit with a buzzer and a single cell.
> Practise drawing circuits here.

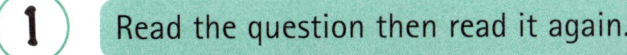

1 Read the question then read it again.

2 Picture the question.

3 Remember the key facts.

4 Work through the problem.

Draw a simple circuit with two bulbs and a battery.

Only use symbols. Do not use drawings.

A series circuit has the two bulbs arranged one after the other.

A switch is on when it looks like this.

It is off when it looks like this.

KEY FACTS   the language

symbols – a way of showing an object with a very simple
diagram that does not look like the real object.

The size of forces

To achieve Level 5 you will need to know about forces of different sizes.
For example: big forces are needed to overcome big forces.

Let's practise!

Question: Kim dragged a box across different surfaces. She used a spring balance to measure the force.

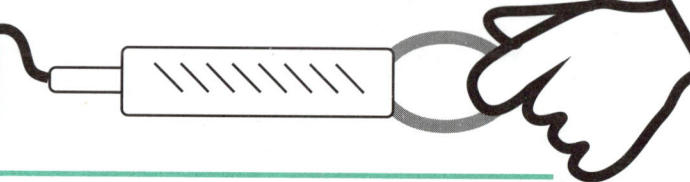

She measured the force needed to move the box.

	Force needed to move box
Pulling on a carpet	10
Pulling on floor tiles	7
Pulling on grass	14

a) What units are used to measure force? _____

b) What force was she having to pull against? _____

c) Why was more force needed to pull over grass? _____

d) Why was less force needed to pull over floor tiles? _____

1 Read the question then read it again.

2 Picture the question. What do you know?

3 Remember the key facts.

The question is in parts. Answer each part separately.

Think about a spring balance. What are the units?

The force Kim is pulling against is friction. The rougher the surface, the more friction there is.

KEY FACTS   the language

force – a pull or push

friction – the force that works against movement

newtons – the units used to measure force

Weighing in air and water

Achieved?

To achieve Level 5 you will need to be able to measure forces and explain the results. For example: the forces that pull on an object in and out of water.

Let's practise!

Question: Paul weighed a brick using a forcemeter. He found it had a pull of 14 newtons. He dangled the brick into a bucket of water. He used the forcemeter to measure the pull. He found the pull was now only 9 newtons.

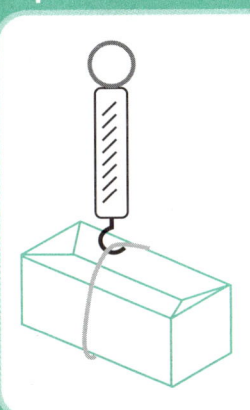

a) What force was pulling the brick down? _____

b) Why did it weigh less when it was hanging in water? _____

1 Read the question then read it again.

The force pulling down pulls with a force of 14 newtons. There is another force that partly supports the brick when it is in water.

2 Picture the question.

Draw the brick with arrows to show the direction of the forces pulling and pushing on it.

3 Think of another example.

Normally you cannot lift up a person. In a swimming pool it is easy to support someone until you start to lift them out of the water.

4 Remember the key facts.

Gravity is a force that pulls down. **Upthrust** from the water partly supports objects in water.

KEY FACTS   the language

gravity – the force that pulls all objects towards the Earth.

upthrust – the force that pushes up on objects in water

Air brakes

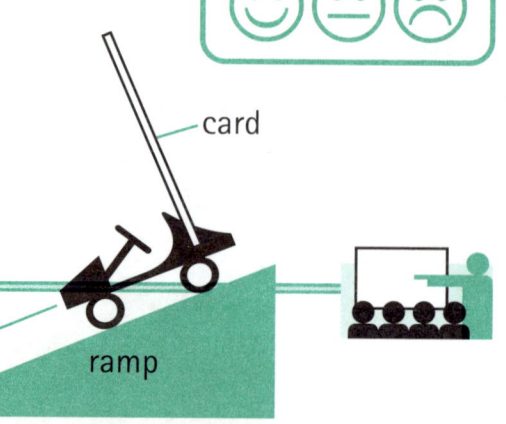
card

ramp

To achieve Level 5 you will need to know the names of forces and the direction they work in.
For example: air resistance is a force that works against the direction of movement.

Let's practise!

Question: Ashleigh let a car roll down a ramp. She measured how far it travelled. She attached a piece of card to the car. She changed the size of the card and measured how far the car went each time.

Explain the pattern of these results. Use the words 'air resistance' in your answer.

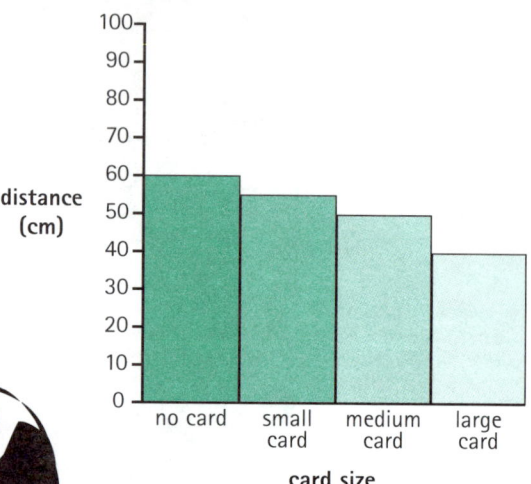

distance (cm)

100
90
80
70
60
50
40
30
20
10
0

no card   small card   medium card   large card

card size

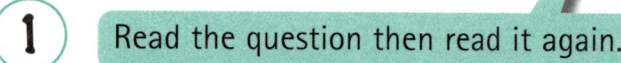

① Read the question then read it again.

② Study the chart.

③ Remember the key facts.

④ Think of other examples.

The chart shows all the information you need.

The bigger the card, the less far the toy car went.

Air resistance is greater with a big area.

If you are running with a large sheet of cardboard, it is more difficult to run quickly if you hold it flat in front of you than if it is by your side.

KEY FACTS

Air resistance can only work on objects that are moving.
This is unlike friction, which works on objects that are still.

Pitch

To achieve Level 5 you will need to know some of the factors involved in the pitch of a sound.
For example: the tighter a string the higher the pitch.

Let's practise!

> **Question: Meena is playing her guitar. She experiments with the ways in which she can change the pitch of the sound.**

a) She slackens the string.
What effect does that have on the pitch of the sound it makes?

b) She puts her finger on the string to make it shorter.
What effect does that have on the pitch of the sound?

c) Explain how the sound reaches Meena's ears.

1 Read the question then read it again.

There are three parts to the question.

2 Picture the question. What do you know?

The string vibrates. The quicker it vibrates, the higher the pitch.

3 Remember the key facts.

- Tight strings have a high pitch.
- Slack strings have a low pitch.
- Short strings have a high pitch.
- Long strings have a low pitch.

4 Think of similar examples.

- Small tuning forks are high pitched.
- Large tuning forks have a low pitch.
- Small (descant) recorders have a high pitch.
- Large (treble) recorders have a low pitch.

5 Work through the problem.

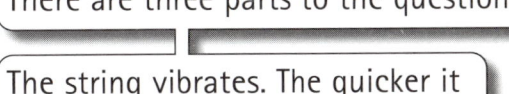

Vibrating string makes the air vibrate and this travels through the air to her ear.

KEY FACTS   the language

vibrate – something that moves backwards and forwards

pitch – the measure of how low or high a note is

How we see things

To achieve Level 5 you will need to know how light
is reflected off surfaces to reach our eyes.
For example: how light is bounced of mirrors.

Let's practise!

Question: Draw two arrows to show how the
light from the bulb reaches the person's eye.

mirror

① Read the question then read it again.

② Remember the key facts.

③ Think about other examples.

You have to draw two arrows. Lines
without arrowheads will not be enough.

The light comes from the source and hits
the mirror. It then bounces off the mirror
into the person's eye.

Light comes from a source and is
reflected off this book into your
eyes. Which is the main light
source in your room now?

KEY FACTS   the language

source – the object that gives off light

reflect – bounce off

The difference between reflections and shadows

To achieve Level 5 you will need to know that a shadow is a place where light is blocked off. Reflections are formed when light bounces off an object.

Hold your hand out in front of you. You can see it because light bounces off it into your eyes.

There is probably a shadow where your hand is blocking light.

Let's practise!

Question: This boy is looking at an apple.

a) Draw the shadow of the apple where it falls on the square of paper in the diagram.

b) Use arrows to show the way the light is reflected to the boy so he can see the apple.

1 Read the question then read it again.

2 Do something similar.

3 Remember the key facts.

There are two parts to the question.

Draw a simple object like a rubber or pencil sharpener. Label the shadow and the reflected light.

Shadow is where light is blocked. Reflection is where light is bounced off.

★ Tip

Look at a polished object, like a steel kettle or pan. Look at the reflections and look at the shadows it casts.

Shadows

To achieve Level 5 you will need to know how shadows are formed.

Let's practise!

Question: Pat and Gary are making shadows using their heads. Gary says this sort of shadow is called a silhouette. Gary measures the distance that Pat is from the projector. He measures the height of the shadow made by Pat's head. The two boys draw a graph.

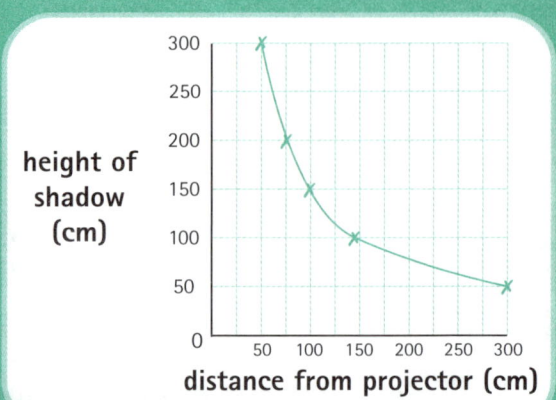

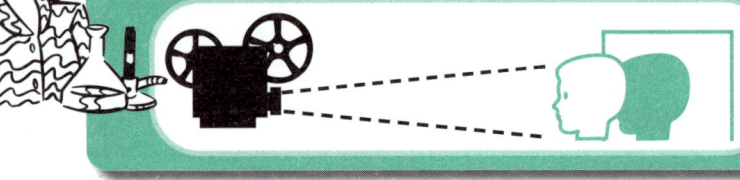

a) What was the size of Pat's shadow when he was 100 cm from the projector?

_____

b) What happens to the size of Pat's shadow as he gets closer to the projector?

_____

1 Read the question then read it again.

You only need to give one measurement to answer the first question. Now read the second question. You need to look for the pattern.

2 Picture the problem.

Draw a sketch of the projector, Pat and the wall or screen. Try to draw it like a plan. Draw it with Pat very close to the wall and then again with him far away. This will help you work out in which position most light is blocked off. Now you can work out the pattern.

3 Look at the graph.

Put your finger on any point on the line. The bottom axis shows how far away the object is from the projector. The side axis shows the size of the shadow.

4 Remember the key facts.

Shadows are made where light is cut off by an object. The size of the shadow gets bigger as the object gets closer to the projector.

5 Check your answer.

The shadow can never be smaller than Pat's head.

The movement of the Sun

Achieved?

To achieve Level 5 you will need to know about the effects caused by the movement of the Earth.

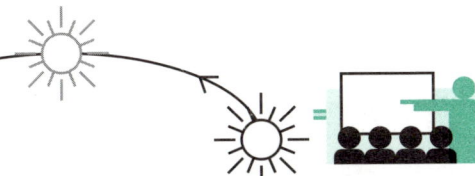

Let's practise!

Question: Each day the Sun rises in the east. Each day it sets in the west. Explain why this happens.

1 Read the question then read it again.

Do not simply describe what happens. You should try to explain why.

2 Picture the question.

Remember that you live on a huge turning ball. If you are looking 'down' towards the equator then the Sun rises to your left. It sets to your right.

3 Remember the key facts.

The Sun appears to move only because the Earth is turning on its axis.

Question: The length of shadows changes during the day. Explain why this happens.

1 Picture the question.

Think of the shadows in your playground that you see at different times of day.

2 Remember the key facts.

The Sun appears to move across the sky. It is the Earth that turns. When the Sun rises it is low in the sky. The shadows are long.
During the day it rises higher. The shadows become shorter.
Past midday the Sun gets lower in the sky. The shadows become longer.

KEY FACTS   the language

midday – middle of the day (around noon or 1pm)

Sun – the star that gives us heat and light

axis – an imaginary stick through the Earth around which it rotates

The year

At Level 5 you should be able to describe the movement of the Earth.
For example: the Earth's orbit movement that gives us a year.

Let's practise!

Question: This diagram shows the Earth and Sun. Add an arrow to show the way the Earth orbits the Sun. How long does it take the Earth to make a complete orbit of the Sun?

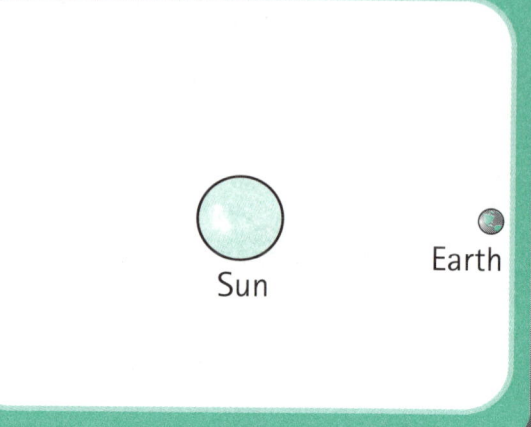

Sun   Earth

1 Read the question then read it again.

Draw the arrow showing the orbit of the Earth around the Sun. Do not confuse this with the way the Earth spins on its own axis.

2 Picture the question.

The orbit of the Earth is around the Sun. You are looking down on the Earth from above the north pole.

3 Remember the key facts.

The Sun is the centre of the Solar System. It is actually moving but for this question we can imagine that it stays still. The Earth spins on its axis and orbits the Sun along with the other eight planets.

4 Work through the problem.

The Earth takes one year to orbit the Sun.

5 Check your answer.

It takes the Earth six months to get halfway around its orbit.

KEY FACTS   the language

orbit – to circle round another object

spin – to turn on its own axis

year – the time taken for the Earth to make a complete orbit of the Sun

 Tip

The Earth orbits the Sun in an anticlockwise direction.

A year on the planet Mercury is only 88 days long because it is much closer to the Sun and its orbit is shorter. However, a year on Uranus is many Earth years long because it is further from the Sun than the Earth is and its orbit is longer.

Predicting

To achieve Level 5 you will need to use results of experiments to help predict what is likely to happen.
For example: you should use a line graph to predict how quickly sugar will dissolve in water of a particular temperature.

Let's practise!

Question:

a) How long did it take the sugar to dissolve in water at 60 °C?

_____

b) How long do you think it will take the sugar to dissolve in water at 70 °C?

_____

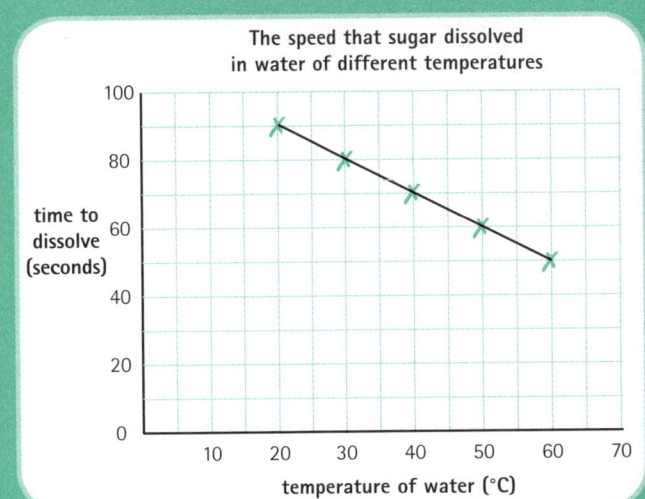

The speed that sugar dissolved in water of different temperatures

time to dissolve (seconds)

temperature of water (°C)

c) What does this line graph tell you about the way sugar dissolves in water? _____

1. Read the question then read it again. → You need to use the information on the graph.

2. Picture the question. What does it tell you? → The time taken for sugar to dissolve depends on the temperature of the water.

3. Think about everyday examples. → Sugar dissolves quickly in hot tea but takes a long time to dissolve in a cold drink.

4. Work through the problem for (a). → Look along the bottom of the graph until you reach 60 °C. Go straight up until you hit the line. Look across to the number on the side axis.

5. Work through the problem for (b). → Continue the graph line downwards until it reaches the line above 70 °C. Look across to the number on the side axis.

KEY FACTS   the language

dissolve – mix a solid and a liquid until you cannot see the solid at all
temperature – a measure of how hot something is

Explaining results

To reach Level 5 you will need to be able to explain the results of tests.

Let's practise!

Question: Sami and Leon made parachutes of different sizes and attached a weight to them. They used the same weight each time. They tested how quickly the parachutes fell.
Here are their results:

Size of the parachute (cm^2)	Drop 1	Drop 2	Drop 3	Average (seconds)
400	3.2	4.5	4.0	3.8
300	2.9	2.9	3.2	3.0
200	2.6	2.6	2.6	2.6
100	2.4	2.6	2.5	2.5

a) Why did Sami and Leon do each test three times?

b) What was the average time taken for the 200 cm^2 parachute to fall?

c) Explain these results.

1 Read the question then read it again.

The answer is in the table.
The final column is an average.

2 Picture the question.

Did changing the parachute size have an effect on the speed of fall?

3 Remember the key facts.

Air resistance slows objects that move through the air. The bigger the object, the more air resistance there is.

4 Work through the problem.

They did the test three times to check that their results were reliable. The average for the 200 cm^2 parachute was 2.6 seconds. The bigger the parachute, the slower it fell. This is because there is more air resistance acting on a bigger parachute.

KEY FACTS   the language

average – you work out the mean (a type of average) by adding the times for each drop and dividing by the number of drops

air resistance – the force that slows down objects that are moving through the air

Using evidence to reach a conclusion

Achieved?

To reach Level 5 you will need to use evidence to reach a conclusion.
For example: making connections between sets of information.

Let's practise!

Question: Ali and Louise looked for minibeasts in different habitats. They made a table of results.

	In the soil of the flower bed	Under the hedge	Under stones	On the rose bushes
	Damp soil	Dry soil	Damp and dark	In the open
greenfly	0	0	0	34
worms	4	0	6	0
spiders	1	2	1	2
ants	0	lots	0	3
slugs	1	0	4	0

Tick the correct conclusions.

a) Worms live in damp places.

b) Spiders are adaptable and can be found in a number of different places.

c) Slugs can only live under stones.

d) It is too dry under the hedge for anything to live there.

e) Ants eat greenfly.

1 Read the question then read it again.

2 Picture the question. What does it tell you?

3 Remember the key facts.

4 Work through the problem.

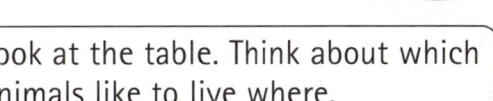

Look at the table. Think about which animals like to live where.

The children looked in four different places for minibeasts.

Try to use only the evidence from the table and do not add anything you think you know about these minibeasts.

Tick the correct conclusions.

KEY FACTS   the language

habitat – place where an animal or plant lives

adapted – suited to the environment of a habitat

environment – the conditions of a habitat

Evaluating experiments

To reach Level 5 you will need to be able to say whether your experiments were good ones.
For example: you should be able to suggest ways in which experiments could be improved.

Let's practise!

Question: Rashid did an experiment to see how high a ball bounces. Rashid said: "The red ball bounces best. My results show that large balls bounce better than small ones."

	carpet	wood floor
red ball (large ball)	30 cm	50 cm
blue ball (small ball)	40 cm	45 cm

a) How could Rashid have improved his test?

_____

b) Were his conclusions correct?

_____

1 Read the question then read it again.

2 Picture the question. What does it tell you?

3 Study the table.

4 Remember the key facts.

5 Check your answer.

Do you think he did enough tests? Did he need to work out an average? Do his results look believable?

He only did each test once. He thinks that the red ball is the best bouncer because it did the highest bounce.

The blue ball was the best bouncer on the carpet but the red one was best on the wood floor. If you add the two values together then the blue ball is best overall.

Try to repeat readings if possible so that you have an average for each surface and each ball.

Rashid should have done more tests and worked out an average to check his results.

★ Tip

Always repeat measurements.

Make sure the results really support your conclusion.

Making sense of line graphs

To achieve Level 5 you will need to be able to interpret line graphs.
For example: this line graph shows the time that a candle burns in jars of different sizes.

Let's practise!

Question:

a) How long would the candle burn for in a jar of 250 ml?

   _____

b) How long would you expect it to burn for in a jar of 600 ml?

   _____

c) Is it true that a candle will burn twice as long in a jar that has twice the volume? Explain your answer.

   _____

d) If you used a candle with a smaller flame in this experiment, what difference would you expect? Explain your idea.

   _____

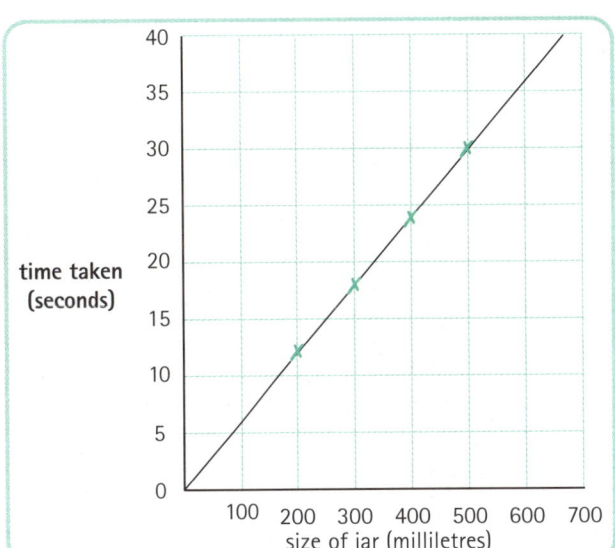

time taken (seconds) / size of jar (millilitres)

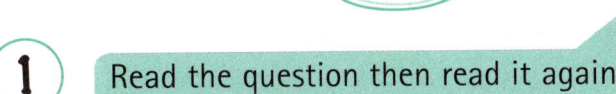
1 Read the question then read it again.

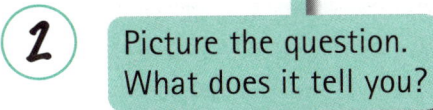
2 Picture the question. What does it tell you?

3 Study the last question.

4 Remember the key facts.

Look at the graph. It shows a steady increase in the length of time that the candle will burn for.

The candle in the jar uses up the air. Bigger jars contain more air than smaller jars.

The rate at which the flame uses air depends on the size of the flame. This means that smaller flames will last longer than bigger flames.

Candles burn the wax. They need air to do this. The jar fills up with the gases given off by the burning wax.

Using line graphs to make predictions

To reach Level 5 you will need to be able to draw and interpret line graphs.

Let's practise!

Question: Sophia and Harry used sensors attached to a computer to see what happened to the temperature of water in four different cans. Each can started with very hot water. They ran the experiment for 60 minutes. The computer drew four separate lines on the screen.

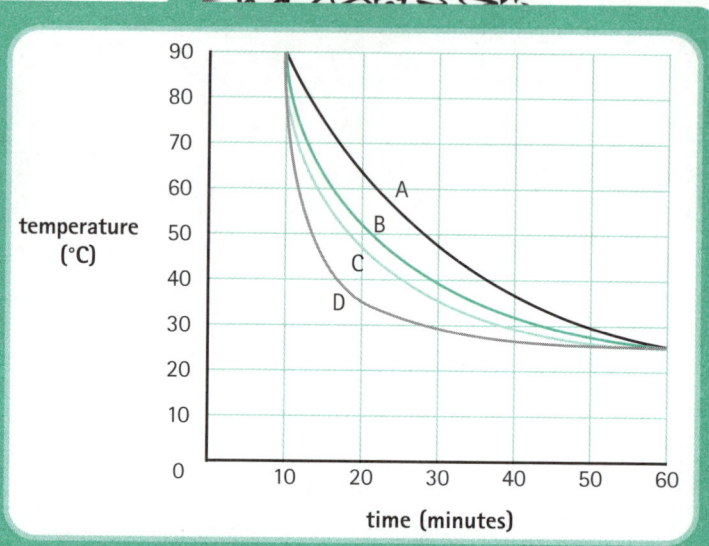

a) Which can cooled quickest?

b) Which can cooled slowest?

c) Which can probably did not have any insulation covering it?

d) Which can probably had the thickest and best insulation?

1 Read the question then read it again.

Look at the graph to see which line shows the can that cooled quickest.

2 Picture the question. What does it tell you?

The temperature sensors take the temperature of each can at the same time and draw the lines for each one.

3 Study the questions and think about the cans.

The one that cooled quickest must have had the worst insulation.

4 Remember the key facts.

Materials that help insulate slow down the movement of heat.

KEY FACTS   the language

thermal insulator – a material that slows the movement of heat

temperature sensor – a thermometer attached to a computer

KEY FACTS Sc1

At Level 4 you need to be able to:

* see that you need evidence to support scientific ideas
* decide on the best way to do an experiment or test
* make good predictions
* select the most important information
* choose the best equipment for a test
* record observations and measurements
* draw and make sense of a bar chart
* come to conclusions
* say ways in which work can be improved

At Level 5 you need to be able to:

* explain scientific ideas
* choose the best information
* choose the right equipment to make measurements
* use the equipment correctly
* repeat measurements
* explain why there might be differences between measurements of the same thing
* understand line graphs
* draw line graphs
* suggest ways in which work could be improved
* use scientific ways to communicate ideas

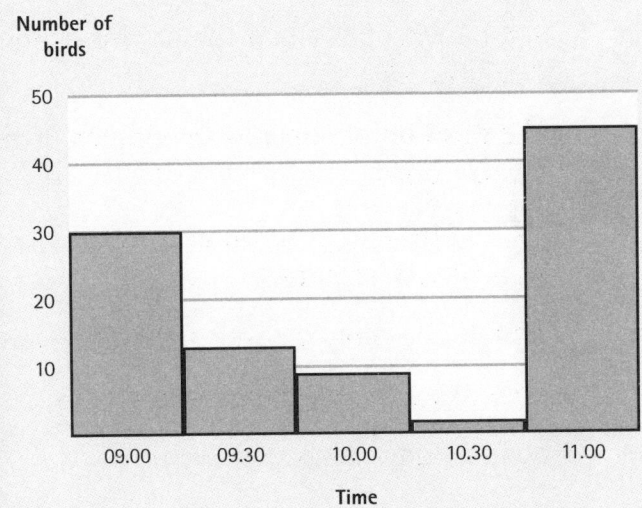

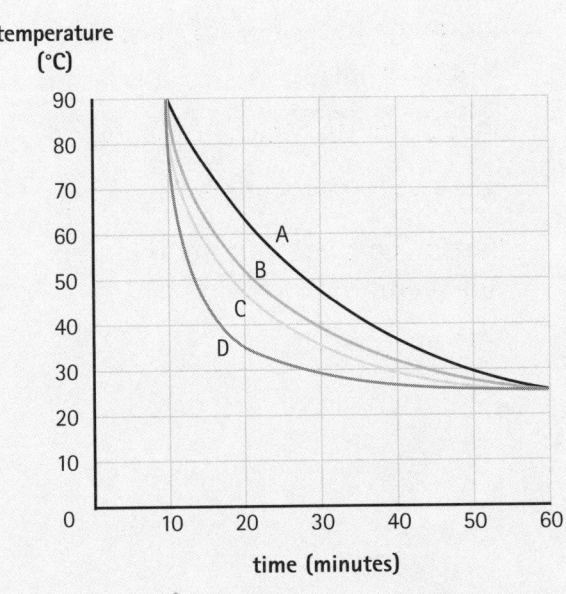

KEY FACTS   Sc2

At Level 4 you need to know:

★ the names of some of the organs of the human body

★ the position of some of the organs of the human body

★ the names and position of some of the organs of a variety of plants

★ how to use simple keys to identify living things

★ how to put living things into groups

★ about food chains

At Level 5 you need to know:

★ the jobs done by some of the organs in the human body

★ the jobs done by some of the organs in plants

★ about the life cycles of humans and some other animals

★ about the life cycles of plants

★ how to classify some living things

★ that living things are found in places that suit them

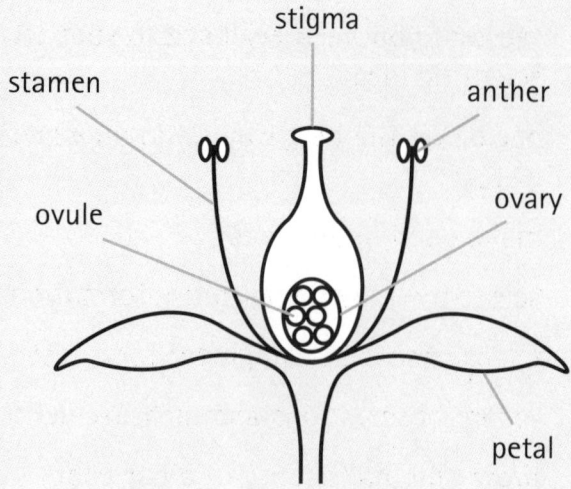

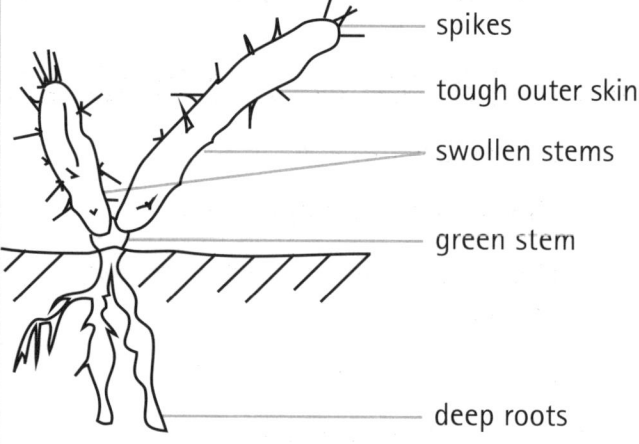

KEY FACTS   Sc3

At Level 4 you need to know:

⭐ about the properties of materials

⭐ how materials are classified into solids, liquids and gases

⭐ how to separate simple mixtures

⭐ the scientific words used to describe changes, such as condense, evaporate and freeze

⭐ which changes are easily reversed and which changes are difficult to reverse

At Level 5 you need to know:

⭐ the properties of metals

⭐ the ways in which metals differ from other solids

⭐ the ways in which changes, such as evaporation and condensation, take place

⭐ how to separate mixtures of materials

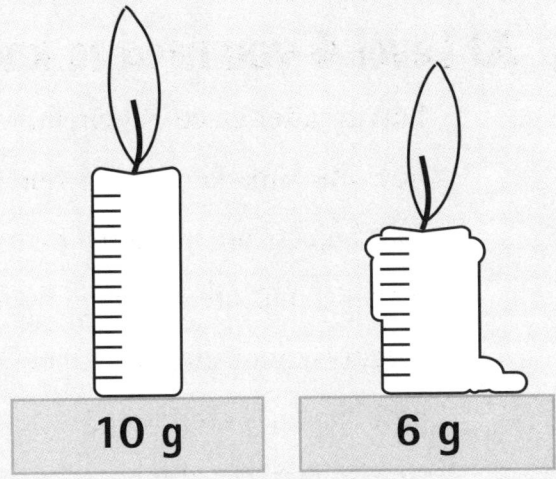

KEY FACTS   Sc4

At Level 4 you need to know:

★ how to alter electrical circuits

★ how the Sun changes position during the day

★ that objects are attracted by gravity

★ which things are attracted by magnets

★ magnets can attract and repel each other

★ how shadows are formed

★ that sounds travel through a variety of materials

At Level 5 you need to know:

★ how to alter the current flowing in a circuit

★ about the effect of adding bulbs to a series circuit

★ about the effects of adding and subtracting batteries from a circuit

★ how to measure forces

★ that forces operate in particular directions

★ how to draw circuits using symbols

★ how to change the pitch and loudness of a sound

★ that vibrations result in sounds

★ that the light from objects passes into your eyes

★ about the orbit of the Earth and the Moon

★ how to use knowledge of orbits to explain the length of the day and year

battery

bulb

switch

buzzer

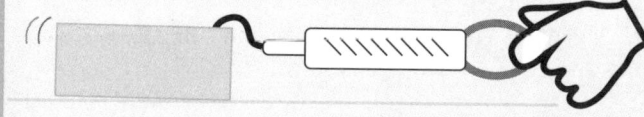

ANSWERS

Page 10
The ink must have travelled up the stem to the flower.

Page 11
Heat must travel up the metal and plastic spoons. The hotter spoon must be made of a good thermal conductor. Wood is not a good thermal conductor.

Page 12
They let the water from the seawater evaporate and leave just the salt.

Page 13
Sara is right because friction is stopping the car from moving. It cannot be air resistance as that acts only when something is moving.

Page 14
The red and blue poles are unlike. Unlike magnetic poles attract.
Both red poles are alike. Like magnetic poles repel.
Both blue poles are alike. Like poles repel.

Page 15
Iron and steel are the metals that are magnetic.

Page 16
Most birds were in the playground at 11:00. Fewest birds were in the playground at 10:30.

Page 17
The distance travelled depends on the height of the ramp. At the highest ramp, the car must have bumped onto the table when it left the ramp and this must have slowed it down.

Page 18
a) The pattern of results shows that the further back you pull the band, the further the car travels.
b) 56 cm was a mistake.
c) It was higher than the others at the same pullback. It travelled even further than the 4 cm pullback.

Page 19
Shefqat – compost/temperature
Julie – type of exercise
Tim – all

Page 20
Heart pumps blood around the body. This carries oxygen to all parts of the body.
Lungs draw in air.
The brain controls movement and thinking.

Page 21
1 Stigma – the female part of the flower that gathers in the pollen.
2 Stamen – produces the pollen.
3 Ovary – holds the seeds or ovules.
4 Petal – Attracts insects to the flower which then pollinate the flower.

Page 22
Katy is right.
Sanjay missed out the fact that the blood goes back to the heart before going out to the body again.
Jake missed out the fact that after the blood comes from the body it goes back to the heart before going to the lungs.

Page 23
The girl's heart rate goes up for one minute, then stays at 130 beats per minute for 5 minutes before coming back to rest after 2 minutes.
The heart beats faster when the body needs more oxygen and food – if it is exercising. It drops back down when the person stops exercising.

Page 24
Eggs – the butterfly starts as an egg. These are laid outside the mother butterfly's body.
Caterpillar – the butterfly is born from the egg as a caterpillar.
Pupa – The caterpillar makes a covering around itself while it changes into an adult butterfly.
Adult – the butterfly emerges from the pupa as an adult. It lays eggs and dies.

Page 25
1 Germination of seed
2 Growing plant
3 Flowering
4 Pollination
5 Development of seeds
6 Dispersal of seeds

Page 26
A – Ash
B – Lime

Page 27
Mammal – human, cow
Bird – seagull, penguin
Reptile – lizard, snake
Amphibian – toad, frog
Fish – shark, pike

Page 28
Woodlice are small animals that need damp and dark conditions. They feed on rotting plants.

Page 29
Tough outer skin to stop water evaporating.
Spikes to stop animals eating the plant.
Deep roots to get water from the soil.
Green stem to make food.
Swollen stems to store water.

Page 30
Before the trees have leaves there is enough light,
water and minerals for the small plants beneath
them. Once the leaves come out the tree blocks out
the light and uses most of the water and minerals.

Page 31
Melt then burn – sugar, cheese, nylon
Burn without melting – cotton, paper
No change – salt

Page 32
The salt dissolved in the water.
Baking powder and vinegar are making a gas.
Mixing vinegar with baking soda.

Page 33
In the jar on the radiator, most water had evaporated.
In the jar in the cool place, least water had
evaporated.
Water evaporates when it gets hot. The warmer it is,
the faster the water evaporates.

Page 34
Water vapour changed to liquid water when it cooled
down. When the steam from the bath hit the mirror,
it cooled and formed mist. When the air near the can
cooled, water vapour in the air formed as drips on the
can.

Page 35
Solidify – Jane; Evaporate – John; Melt – Sam

Page 36
Kate dissolved the coffee in water. She then filtered
the sand and coffee solution and then let the water
evaporate, leaving the coffee behind.

Page 37
A and C. Iron is sample A. Gold is sample C.

Page 38
Stainless steel. Steel and aluminium. It is strong and
light. Because it is too expensive.

Page 39
Because some of the candle has evaporated as a gas.
The wax burned and gas was released. This is a
chemical change which is difficult to reverse.

Page 40
Julie. When a fuel burns it produces new materials.
These new materials are gases.

Page 41

Page 42
a) Newtons
b) Friction
c) Grass is uneven and rough. It has more friction
force.
d) Floor tiles are smoother and have less friction force
than grass or carpet.

Page 43
a) Gravity.
b) It weighed less because upthrust force was
supporting the brick in the water.

Page 44
The larger the card the more air resistance there is.
This slows the car and stops it travelling so far.

Page 45
a) It lowered the pitch of the sound.
b The pitch is higher with a shorter string.
c) The vibrations in the string vibrate the air and this
vibration travels to Meena's ear.

Page 46

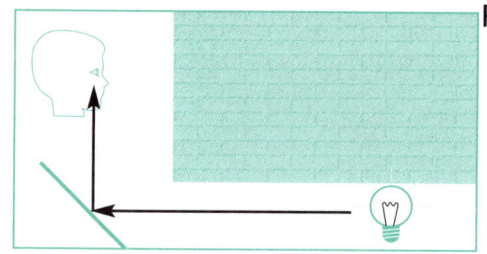

Page 47

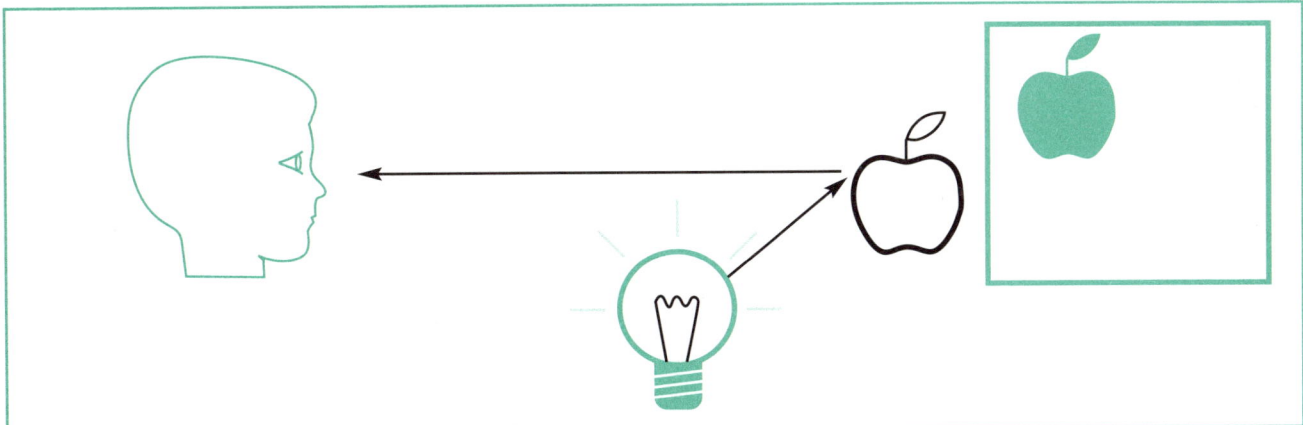

Page 48
150 cm. The size of the shadow gets bigger as it gets closer to the projector.

Page 49
The Sun rises in the east when you look because the Earth is rotating anti-clockwise on its axis.
During the day, the Sun appears to rise in the sky and therefore the shadows are shorter. In the afternoon, the Sun appears to get lower and the shadows get longer again.

Page 50
Arrow should show anti-clockwise direction of the Earth's orbit.
365¼ days or 1 year.

Page 51
a) 50 seconds
b) 40 seconds
c) The warmer the water, the faster the sugar dissolves.

Page 52
a) To check their results were reliable.
b) 2.6 seconds
c) The bigger the parachute, the slower it fell because more air resistance was acting on the bigger parachute.

Page 53
Worms live in damp places; Spiders are adaptable and can be found in a number of different places

Page 54
a) He could do each test more than once to improve the reliability; he could test more surfaces; he could test more balls.
b) No, because the small ball bounced better on the carpet.

Page 55
a) 14–16 seconds
b) 36–37 seconds
c) Yes, because there is more air to burn in a bigger jar.
d) Smaller flames will last longer than bigger flames because they use less air.

Page 56
a) D   b) A   c) D   d) A

Rising Stars UK Ltd., 76 Farnaby Road, Bromley, BR1 4BH

www.risingstars-uk.com

Every effort has been made to trace copyright holders and obtain
their permission for the use of copyright material. The authors and
publishers will gladly receive information enabling them to rectify
any error or omission in subsequent editions.

All facts are correct at time of going to press.

First published 2002
Reprinted 2003
New Edition 2003
Reprinted 2004

Text, design and layout © Rising Stars UK Ltd.

Editorial: Tanya Solomons

Cover design: Burville Riley

Design: Ken Vail Graphic Design, Cambridge

Illustrations: Burville Riley, Beehive Illustration (Theresa Tibbetts)
and Jim Eldridge

Cover photo © Digital Vision/Getty images

British Library Cataloguing in Publication Data
A CIP record for this book is available from the British Library.

ISBN 1-904591-09-4

Printed by Wyndeham Gait, Grimsby, UK